EUROPEAN TRUCKS

EUROPEAN TRUCKS

On the road in Europe in colour

David Jacobs

Osprey Colour Series

Published in 1983 by Osprey Publishing Limited
12–14 Long Acre, London WC2E 9LP
Member company of the George Philip Group

British Library Cataloguing in Publication Data

Jacobs, David
    European trucks.—(Colour paperback)
    1. Motor-trucks
    I. Title
    629.2′24   TL230
ISBN 0-85045-489-1

Editor Tim Parker

Designed by Norman Brownsword

Printed in Hong Kong

Anyone with the experience to compare the world of the trucker in North America with that of Great Britain and Europe over the recent past cannot have failed to notice how they are moving together. Ten years ago they were poles apart, today they are really quite close. *EUROPEAN TRUCKS*, through the medium of 120 colour photographs all taken by David Jacobs, shows you just where the European scene is.

Undeniably *EUROPEAN TRUCKS* follows in the footsteps of *AMERICAN TRUCKS* and *AMERICAN TRUCKS 2* (by David Jacobs) both of which have been roaring successes. Coming after the American books obviously places the European truck in its right perspective. The European truck probably leads in technology and efficiency but the American truck pulls ahead on glamour and excitement, or does it? The photographs within are specially selected to show off just how well the Europeans can pamper their wagons (the word lorry is apparently sadly disappearing). David Jacobs has combed Britain and Northern Europe to offer a wide variety of make and model in their appropriate scenic work places. His skill does justice to Europe's Wild West. Enjoy his enthusiasm and art.

Yet another self-portrait of photographer David Jacobs. Yet again David has to thank all the truck drivers whose trucks appear within these pages and his close friends Lizzy, Bernard, Sue W, Tony Murray, Fred and Syd!

Contents

Spoiler

LEFT Painted in Italian national colours this Fiat rigid with cab spoiler appears to be nearly out of control some 20 miles north of Milan

ABOVE Another Fiat three axle rigid sports turbo power and another style of cab spoiler. It's on display at Battersea, London, for the Historic Commercial Vehicle Society's Brighton Run in 1982

ABOVE Another spoiler, another Fiat.
Battersea again for the Brighton Run.
Openings in the spoiler front are unusual

LEFT Pegaso tractor at rest near Dijon in
northern France. Its spoiler is not so
sophisticated. At least it makes room for
display signwriting

French registered Mercedes-Benz 1933
displays a cunning 'short' spoiler mounted
close to the trailer refridgeration motor
(also British RAC and AA badges).
Weather suggests Watford Gap on the M1
motorway

Mercedes-Benz 'double' near Leiden in
Holland with relatively ineffective spoiler
and two gnomes

Two Brain Volvos in convoy show
concern for efficiency and cleanliness. Yet
another style of spoiler

LEFT A little bit of 'nearly custom' on this Italian registered Scania 142M. Truck's on its way through Germany south to Austria near Munich. Spoiler has paint you can't see

ABOVE Daf at Scratchwood, the M1's first service area going north from London. Spoiler angle differs again

Conventional

ABOVE Heavyweight lowloader, American style. Two Renault GBH280s near Dijon in France. 'Normal control' cabs are still in fashion for certain jobs in Europe, less so in the UK

LEFT Scammell Contractor specially converted to wrecker. Appropriately known as *The Hulk*, this type of tractor is best known in its role as tank transporter. Here it's on show in Gillingham at a charity show

Heavy hauliers Wynns' Scammell Contractor called *Cavalier* tops close to 20 mph and averages but 7 with its total length of 123 feet. Today it's a clay chimney for Blue Circle Industries, the 'cement people'

ABOVE A Belgian registered conventional Scania 110 Super comes into Dover. Plain and simple

LEFT 'Miniature American double rig', perhaps. A Scania L76 tanker waits to dump fuel near St Gotthard. The Swiss appear to maintain their trucks for many more years than normal

ABOVE Big brother. Another Scania conventional with sleeper cab at film-blurring speed going south from Dijon on the autoroute. Just as plain, and just as simple

RIGHT N12 Volvo with a Turbo 6 under the bonnet powering out of Lugano towards Italy, but not home

ABOVE Remember the white Scania.
Same place, same time but Volvo's version
and without a trailer. It's their newest
normal control cab and it looks to be on
delivery

RIGHT Swiss made Berna (badged and
look-alike Suarer) have charm all of their
own. Location, St Moritz

Paint

ABOVE Conservative and modest, but
typically British is this signwritten trailer.
No mistaking who's running this Volvo
F1017 rig. M1 service area, Scratchwood

LEFT Beautiful paint job, to the standards
of the best Americans. F series Volvo
sleeper cab has lots of paint area which
can benefit. It's Dutch registered

ABOVE A pair of Leyland Crusaders in the British Army's best 'spit and polish'. These REME promotion vehicles are finished to the very highest standards. Is that a CB twig poking up there?

RIGHT Leaning Tower of Pisa on the A1 in Leicestershire. Clever idea for some haulier of Italian produce

30

LEFT Close to custom. This French registered GMC Astro imported from Michigan hauls meat. It's nicely not 'over the top' as it rests in North London. Rare sight

BELOW More meat. Handsome, careful painting by a signwriter rather than strong customizing by an air brush wizard. Sunday, close to London's Smithfield Market

Volvo's latest sleeper shot in Holland. Bright but low key paint emphasises haulier's name rather than the quality of the paint. Tony Verdrr's Globetrotter covers just Arnheim, Utrecht and Paris

Nothing special, just careful spraying, for
this Renault R310 in Fontainbleau, France

Too much or is it too little? Japanese
Hino (Toyota owned) comes assembled in
Ireland. Early morning excavator loading
in the Mile End Road, East London

36

Red, cream and green Leyland Roadtrain in typical British style livery. Leyland Vehicles' saviour tilt cab tractor series is becoming very common in the UK if not in Europe

Speed

Traditional European draw bar trailer rig, not so popular in the UK. High speed Scania in Holland. Note careful striping

Sleeperless Scania with spoiler missing from cab roof mounts trundles through the rain clouds in the Dutch flat lands

ABOVE An odd couple. Mercedes-Benz box van and draw bar trailer near Fontainbleau in France

RIGHT Solid efficiency. Scania 112 series tractor on the autoroute at Leiden going north to Amsterdam. Container needs repair and paint

ABOVE High speed wave from ERF driver as he slows for the Scratchwood service area on the M1 just north of London. British 70 mph speed limit is easily breached by this type of modern truck

RIGHT Rare Fiat 643N first built in 1963 comes with 9.16 litre engine. These 640 series trucks are particularly hardy, hence many of them are still on the Italian roads today. Unloaded, this Milan registered 4 ×2 is fast

ABOVE Driver dexterity allows fast entry and exit to produce markets even with large rigs. Unloaded and headed for home

LEFT Swiss Saurer D series 8 ×4 tipper doing essential work at St Moritz. Swiss law bans other trucks from the roads at weekends. 12 litre turbo 6 provides the urge

FOLLOWING PAGE Speed blurrs the vision, or is it the rain which does the damage? Scania LB111 rig blasts by towards the St Gotthard tunnel

ABOVE 'Running in. Please pass'. Light weight helps high speed when on trade plates. . . . Ford Cargo on delivery to the body shop

LEFT Unloaded Fiat (rear axle wheels off the road) shows speed in the rain. 684N cab came in 1970 along with other types

Crawl

LEFT Heavy load, steep incline, funnels of diesel smoke for those who pass by. Saurer (Swiss) gets blown by Fiat (Italian) followed by BMW (German) with Fiat and Scánia ready to pounce. All at Castione, Switzerland

ABOVE Ferry ports are always busy and congested. Here a long Volvo tractor/curtain trailer finds leaving Dover slower than expected

ABOVE Not all hitchhikers are lucky. Even at less than crawling speed and plenty of room to stop the Continental truck driver is wary. Orange Mercedes

RIGHT Same spot but a much less common truck. Lancia trucks have been made by Fiat since 1969 – this one's obviously a Fiat look alike – as have Unics. Fiat also work through OM and Magirus-Deutz too

ABOVE Deutz 320PK in traffic in Holland.
Cab roof running lights and twin trumpet
horns seem to be pretty standard these
days

RIGHT London's famous Blackwall
Tunnel. Sunday afternoon so relative
peace for this Daf on the south side. It's
probably heading for Dover and
continental Europe

Belgian registered Scania 112H refrigerated
van in the early morning in North
London

ABOVE Same early morning but a Leyland Marathon 2 close to the City of London near Old Street. Could be carrying anything but its likely destination is the Port of London, even the south coast

FOLLOWING PAGE Austrian backdrop: Mercedes-Benz short wheelbase tipper towing a lowloader trailer, a fairly unusual rig even for the Innsbruck area where manoeuvrability is of prime importance

57

Mile End Road, through the City of London, in the early morning. Throttle hard down, in low gear, heaving on the wheel

Mercedes and Mercedes. The car speeds
through the rain whilst the truck waits to
deliver fuel to the filling station in
Switzerland. Every driver appreciates
Mercedes quality

Owner/operator Jan Vanlommel slows his
142M Scania, all of 16 metres long in
Fontainbleau, France. He travels Greece/
Belgium with meat and fruit

One of a fleet of wreckers, this one's a Daf,
which hauls off the M1 close to London.
It's a specialist business where care is
needed

ABOVE Uncluttered Scania sits during maintenance in an Amsterdam truck garage. Note new cab sitting in the background. With the obviously easy to remove tilting cab accident repairs can be quick and relatively cheap by simply renewing the cab

LEFT The tilting cab is an ingenious idea for all forward control or cabover trucks now considered essential for easy, fast maintenance. The traditional normal control truck, of course, doesn't need it

This sad looking container truck took six
hours to right using air bags and holding
ropes. Damage was relatively light. Central
London is no place to park like this,
however

Rest

ABOVE The same Vanlommel Scania again.
This time stationary. Driver has mastered
the subtle art of European customizing for
Anne–Marie even though there are hints
of American influence

RIGHT Stark contrast. Opposite St Pauls
Cathedral one Sunday asleep. This ERF
is waiting to pick up a refrigerated
container from the nearby London
wholesale meat market at Smithfields

ABOVE Apart from *Able*, no identification
for this rig at the Watford Gap service
area, the M1 'half way house' between
London and Birmingham. It's another
Scania

RIGHT Handsome ERF C40, new in 1982.
Commendable attempt to integrate the
paintwork with the style and purpose of
the rig. ERF have been successful in the
heavyweight arena

68

Serious paint. Although after the style of
the cabovers in North America this pair of
British registered trucks have succeeded
with a uniform and bright colour scheme.
No mistaking the Leyland and Ford
origins

Virtually unseen outside Austria and
Germany, the Steyr range is non the less
very popular in Austria where they are
made. 91 series uses tilt cab dating back to
1968 in concept. Driver asleep

Black and handsome. Scania rests off the
M20 near to Sheerness on the way to (or
from ?) Dover

F88 Volvo, unadorned but clean and
simple too, just waits

ABOVE Awake. Dave Birkitt, long distance truck driver. His F88 Volvo takes three weeks round trip to Turkey regularly. Photographed here in the confined space of his sleeper cab

LEFT More waiting. Going on or coming off, doesn't matter. All wait at Dover. Right to left; Fiat, Man, Fiat, Bedford, Fiat, Saurer, Volvo, Scania, Scania, Daf

Work

LEFT Ready to start north. New Alfa Romeos on route from northern Italy up through France to Paris. Motel is just off the autoroute

ABOVE French registered Unic (Fiat) sells fruit in Chablis. This style of truck is very common in the French countryside where produce is sold to the local populace as well as passing tourists

Famous for its air-cooled V8 engine,
Deutz have been building high quality
trucks for years. Here a 232 does sterling
service transporting two 'historic
commercials' for the 1982 Brighton Run.
The green tractor is a Foden of 1942 used
to haul timber

Austrian Man diesel near Koblenz. This
is their standard forward-control series
ranging up to a gross weight of 150 tonnes.
Likely engine of this one is a turbo six
cylinder

Spanish Pegaso 3188, tilt cab with sleeper
and twin steer. Still rare to see anything
other than a Spanish registered Pegaso,
however. American International Harvester
now have a stake in the factory

Enter Dover. Belgian registered Scania
bulk tanker starts the paper work

'Eat more fruit'. Delivery by Bedford TL
in south London

St Moritz Circus Nock. Modern European
fleet for modern European circus

ABOVE Hampstead Heath Fair in the Vale of Health, north London. Truck by Foden

RIGHT Scammell Crusader near Blackheath, south London. Strong bright pillar box red for BRS stalwart

ABOVE Steyr in its homeland, Austria. Short haul delivery as the shadows lengthen

RIGHT *Jack of Diamonds* is the name given to this 401 Seddon Atkinson at a charity fair at Gillingham in Kent. Traditional Atkinson 'A' adorns the cab front once again for this lightweight series

Empty box pallets form the load of this
Dutch Mercedes-Benz rig. Draw bar
trailer gets more common all the time

Nearly horizon. Medway flyover shot from
Chatham

Night

FAR LEFT Scania at dusk in the Alpine foothills

LEFT Volvo and Bass homeward bound

'Transconti' wrecker by Ford

ABOVE Reflections of a cattle truck in France

RIGHT Setting sun on the North Circular, London

Pegaso mirror at Watford Gap!

Ford Transcontinental 4427 at
Smithfields, London

Bedford's new TM series has a Cummins
E–290 diesel in this artic. Tractor unit has
American influence

ABOVE Cold box interior. Up to 1000 lambs can be carried in one of these massive refridgerated containers. Smithfields, London

LEFT White cabover is a rare sight in the UK. Road Commander has aluminium tilt cab. Rig is ready to roll out of north London

Mercedes night light

New Covent Garden in the early morning.
Ford Transconti and beans

Van

ABOVE Dutch style van has coach influence in the cab front. Chassis origins are not obvious, probably Daf, but it could be . . .

LEFT Traditional British style pantechnicon. Bedford Marsden near Cologne on the autobahn. Van appears to be TK based with the egg-box grille

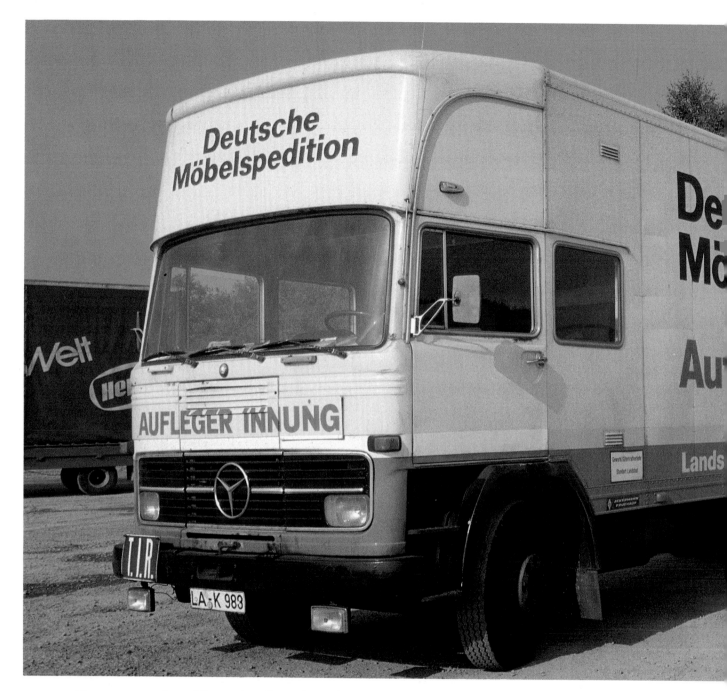

German version. Mercedes-Benz based
box van uses truck front cab panel only.
Everything else is special. Koblenz, West
Germany

ABOVE Simplicity. M–B 1617 box van and
tail-lift rests at Newport Pagnell on the M1

LEFT The Great North Road, as was,
going north through Lincolnshire. Yet
another style of box van (and draw bar
trailer) with specially faired in 'cabover'
effect. Dodge chassis is made in Spain,
ERF in Cheshire

Beer delivery in St Moritz, Switzerland.
New style Steyr is a handsome, home-
brewed outfit

Looks hard worked. No mistaking this
Daf van. Just ordinary

Close-up

ABOVE No doubts. Volvo's Turbo 6

LEFT Heart on its sleeve. Daf 2800 Turbo
Intercooler

ABOVE Four halogen but one wiper; Ford
Transcontinental

RIGHT ABOVE Straight from the signwriter.
Tasteful outlining. Leyland

RIGHT BELOW Bring back the 'A'. So
Seddon Atkinson did

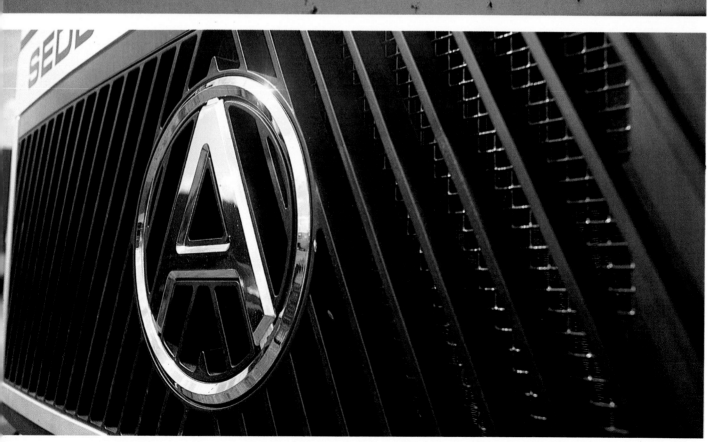

ABOVE Leave the badge on, then spray the stripes

LEFT Spaghetti Junction

ABOVE Luminous paint?

LEFT Scania twig and stack

Visor

ABOVE Typical Dutch custom, this time
on a refuse truck. Visor needs slogan

LEFT Low key cab visor for the square cab
Volvo F12

Familiar Spanish style visor with sign
written Carrasco adorning it. Truck is
Spanish built Dodge 300 series resting at
Scratchwood at the M1's end

Another variation. Unobtrusive for this
F12 Volvo in Holland

ABOVE Curious combination. Spanish style visor on Swiss Saurer. D290 on the left features newer style grille compared with that one about to overtake

RIGHT *King Pip*. Large, aggressive visor for this Yorkshire registered Man shot at Nemours in France. Sun must have been shining a lot

ABOVE Colour coded red. Scania LBS 141 in France

RIGHT Large visor, sleeper cab and proper streamlining both with a roof spoiler but also an integrated side panel system. Scania tractor looks nearly brand new